750

Knots and Splices

Cyrus L Day

Photographs by Bill Beavis
Roger Lee
Mike Peyton

International Marine
Camden, Maine

Published by International Marine®

15 14 13 12 11

Copyright © 1953 by Cyrus L. Day
Published by International Marine, an imprint of
McGraw-Hill, Inc.

Questions regarding the content of this book should
be addressed to:

International Marine
P.O. Box 220
Camden, ME 04843

Questions regarding the ordering of this book
should be addressed to:

The McGraw-Hill Companies
Customer Service Department
P.O. Box 547
Blacklick, OH 43004
Retail customers: 1-800-262-4729
Bookstores: 1-800-722-4726

ISBN 0-07-156378-4

Contents

1 Glossary

BELAY. To make a line fast on a cleat, pin, pair of bitts, or the like.

BELAYING PIN. A wooden or metal pin on which to belay a line.

BEND (noun). A knot used to tie the ends of two free lines together.

BEND (verb). To make fast or to tie, as "to bend two lines together."

BIGHT. (1) The middle of a line; (2) a loop or curve in a line.

BITT. A vertical piece of timber or an iron casting set in the deck for securing hawsers and other lines.

BLOCK. A pully or grooved roller in a casing or shell.

CLEAT. A piece of wood or metal with two arms or horns on which to belay a line.

CROSS TURNS. Turns taken round, and perpendicular to, the turns of a seizing or lashing.

FID. A conical piece of wood (hickory or lignum vitae) for splicing, *etc.*

FRAPPING TURNS. Cross turns (*q.v.*).

HALF-KNOT. The first half of a square knot; identical in structure with an overhand knot.

HAWSER. A rope 5 to 24 inches in circumference, for towing, *etc.*

HEART. A small rope or core in the centre of a hemp or wire rope.

HITCH. A knot used to secure a line to a spar, ring, post, or the like.

KNOT. In general, (1) any fastening, including bends and hitches, made by interweaving cordage. Specifically, (2) a method of tying the ends of two very small cords together, or of forming (3) a noose, (4) a fixed loop, or (5) a knob or stopper.

LAY. The direction (right-handed or left-handed) in which the strands of a rope are twisted; also the tightness (soft, medium common, plain, and hard lay) of the twists.

LINE. A rope used for a particular purpose.

MARL. To bind or secure with a series of marling hitches.

MARLINE SPIKE. A piece of steel, conical and pointed, for splicing, *etc.*

NOOSE. A knot with a loop that binds the closer the more it is drawn.

PALM. A leather mitt with a metal disc in the palm, for pushing sail needles through canvas or rope.

PARCEL. To cover with strips of canvas, for protection against dampness, before serving.

REEF POINTS. Pieces of rope fixed in a sail at regular intervals along a reef band and used in reefing (shortening sail).

REEVE. To pass the end of a line through an opening, hole or block.

RIDERS or **RIDING TURNS.** A second layer of turns in a seizing.

ROPE. Any cord 1 inch or more in circumference and made of vegetable or plastic fibres or of metal wires. The parts of a vegetable-fibre rope are called fibres, yarns and strands. The fibres are usually laid up (twisted) right-handed, the yarns left-handed, and the strands right-handed. Plain-laid or hawser-laid rope has three strands laid up right-handed; shroud-laid rope has four strands laid up right-handed round a heart; cable-laid rope has three plain-laid strands laid up left-handed.

RUNNING KNOT. A noose (*q.v.*).

SEIZING. A lashing for holding two ropes or parts of a rope together. Round seizings have riding turns, flat seizings do not. Racking seizings have figure-eight turns. Throat, middle, quarter, and end seizings are so named from the part of the rope where the seizing is applied.

SERVE. To wind small stuff tightly round a rope, for protection against chafe and dampness.

SHEAVE. A grooved roller in a block.

SINGLE HITCH. Similar to a half hitch, but tied round another object rather than round its own standing part.

SLING. A strap; a loop for hoisting and lowering a man or a load.

SMALL STUFF. Seizing stuff; hemp cordage, generally tarred, of 2, 3, 4, 6 or 9 threads or yarns; hambroline, houseline, marline, roundline, spunyarn, or synthetic twine.

STANDING PART. The main part of a line, as distinguished from the bight (*on* which the knot is tied) and the end (*with* which the knot is tied).

STOP. To lash temporarily with marline or other small stuff.

STOPPER KNOT. A knot to prevent a line from running out through a hole or a block.

STRAP. A sling; small stuff marled together, or a rope with the ends spliced together, for slinging heavy objects. Also spelled "strop."

THIMBLE. A grooved piece of metal, circular or pear-shaped, round which an eye may be spliced in hemp or wire rope.

TOGGLE. A wooden pin on the end of a lashing, either tapered or with a groove round the middle, to act as a stopper.

TWINE. See Small stuff.

WORM. To wind small stuff spirally round in the grooves between the strands of a rope, before parcelling and serving.

2 Basic knots

1. The **HALF HITCH** is a basic element in many knots (see Nos. 9, 18, 27, 34).

2. The **SLIPPED HALF HITCH** can be used instead of No. 1 in knots like Nos. 9 and 34 when quick release is desired. See also Fig. 45c.

3. The **OVERHAND KNOT** or **THUMB KNOT** is the smallest of all knots, and one of the most useful. It forms part of many other knots (see Nos. 23, 24, 25, 41), most of which, however, are landsmen's rather than sailors' knots. It is used as a temporary stopper knot (see Glossary); and it is tied in string, twine, and the like, to prevent the end from fraying. To tie it for this purpose in rope, however, is considered unseamanlike. See Nos. 46 and 47.

4. The **FIGURE-EIGHT KNOT** is better than No. 3 as a stopper knot, because it is bulkier and does not jam so hard.

5. The **REEF KNOT** or **SQUARE KNOT** can be tied when there is tension on both ends. Its proper use is to enclose or bind something, such as a bundle, or a strip of the sail when reefing. It tends to slip if the ropes are of different sizes and materials, and to spill if one of the ends is pulled sharply. Hence it should be used sparingly as a bend (see Glossary), and never as a way to join two hawsers (see Glossary). It consists of two half-knots (see Glossary), one tied on top of the other. The second half-knot should be the reverse of the first, so that the ends *A* and *B* (Fig. 5) will lie alongside their respective standing parts (see Glossary).

6. The **GRANNY KNOT** or **LUBBER'S KNOT** tends to slip or jam, and should be avoided. Note that *A* and *B* do not lie next to the standing parts.

7. The **DRAW KNOT** is a form of the reef knot with one end slipped.

8. The **BOW KNOT** is useful in doing up bundles, tying shoe laces, and whenever quick release, an attractive appearance, and a convenient shortening of the ends are desired. It is a reef knot with both ends slipped.

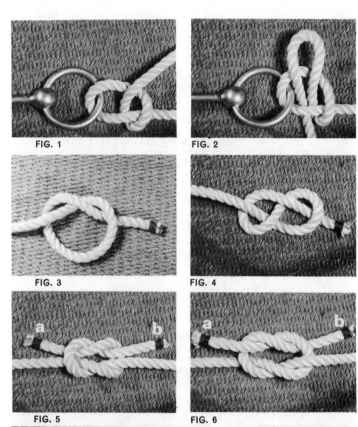

FIG. 1

FIG. 2

FIG. 3

FIG. 4

FIG. 5

FIG. 6

FIG. 7

FIG. 8

3 Bends

9. The **SHEET BEND** or **WEAVER'S KNOT** is the most generally useful bend, ashore or afloat. It holds well with cords or ropes of different diameters and materials, and it is not so readily spilled as the reef knot by means of a quick jerk on the end. Other names for it are simple bend, single bend, common bend and becket bend.

To tie it, cross *A* over *B*, bring *A* down round *B*, and then up again, as shown by the arrow (Fig. 9A). You should do this with a single movement of the right hand, and the result should be a hitch *D* in rope *B* (Fig. 9B), with the end *A* coming up through the hitch. Finally pass *A* round behind *E* and down through *D* (Fig. 9C). Fig. 9D shows how both sides of the finished knot look.

Weavers tie the knot in a quick way by crossing *A* over *B* (Fig. 9E), and grasping the two threads at their intersection with the thumb and forefinger of the left hand. They then take a hitch with the bight of *B* over its own end (Fig. 9F), and put the end of *A* through the hitch thus formed (Fig. 9G).

Both the sheet bend and the reef knot are used to tie the ends of two cords together, yet sailors call one a "bend" and the other a "knot." The distinction is probably due to the difference in function between the two knots. Sailors use the sheet bend to "bend" the ends of two free lines together; they use the reef knot to "tie" or "knot" the ends of a single cord round a bundle or other object.

According to Clifford Ashley, it is dangerous to use the reef knot as a bend. The reader should take note of this warning; and he should also, at this point, study the definition of the word "bend" and the five definitions of the word "knot" in the Glossary.

FIG. 9A

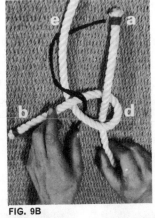

FIG. 9B

FIG. 9C

FIG. 9D

FIG. 9E

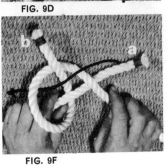

FIG. 9F

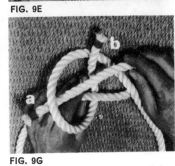

FIG. 9G

10. The **LEFT-HANDED SHEET BEND,** with the ends diagonally opposite each other, has a tendency to slip, and should be avoided.

11. The **DOUBLE SHEET BEND** is a trifle stronger, perhaps, than the single form of the knot (No. 9), and is to be preferred when one line is considerably larger than the other.

12. The **BECKET BEND** is a variation of the sheet bend (No. 9).

13. The **HEAVING-LINE BEND** is used to bend a heaving line to a hawser (see Glossary), or any very small line to a much larger one.

14. The **CARRICK BEND** is a strong, secure bend that cannot jam. Note that it is tied with a regular over-and-under weave, and that the ends should be diagonally opposite each other (Fig. 14A). When pulled taut, the carrick bend "upsets" and falls into two loops (Fig. 14B) which can be readily pried loose with a fid after the knot has been used. All other well-known bends, including the sheet bend (and also the reef knot), tend to jam when the rope is wet and the pull is very great. The carrick bend is, therefore, an indispensable knot, and ought to be better known than it is.

The carrick bend was formerly much used to join hawsers. According to several old manuals of seamanship, the ends of the knot were seized (see Glossary) to the standing parts to prevent the knot from "upsetting" as described above. When the ends are not seized, and when the lines are comparatively small, the "upset" position of the knot is correct and proper (Fig. 14B).

15. The **BOWLINE BEND** is a strong and well-known way to bend two hawsers together. It consists of two interlocking bowlines (No. 18). Although somewhat bulky, it is entirely reliable. The ends should be stopped (see Glossary) to the loops to keep them secure and out of the way.

16. The **STRAP KNOT** holds well in flat material like leather. If tied in rope, it either jams or slips apart with astonishing ease, depending on how the two ends are adjusted.

FIG. 10

FIG. 11

FIG. 12

FIG. 13

FIG. 14A

FIG. 14B

FIG. 15

FIG. 16

13

4 Nooses and loops

17. The **TOGGLE** is a convenient way to join the ends of two lines which may have to be cast off at a moment's notice. Toggles are of various kinds, and are used, for example, in securing circular life preservers to the rails of steamers.

18. The **BOWLINE KNOT** (rhymes with "stolen") is the most useful way to tie a fixed loop in the end of a line. It is simple and strong, and it does not slip or jam.

To tie it, hold the standing part in the left hand, and the end in the right hand. Cross the end over the standing part, and with a flip of the right wrist make a hitch D (called the cuckold's neck) in the standing part, with the end A coming up through it (Fig. 18A). Pass A round behind B and down through D, as shown by the arrow. The whole process is almost precisely as described under No. 9 (the sheet bend), and illustrated in Figs. 9A, 9B and 9C. Indeed the sheet bend and the bowline are structurally identical. The finished bowline appears in Fig. 18B.

The left-handed form of the knot (Fig. 18C) seems to be equally strong and secure, but is not often used. There are many ways to tie the bowline, and it has many uses. It is an indispensable knot.

19. The **BOWLINE ON THE BIGHT** is tied in the middle or bight of a line, when both ends are inaccessible, and when the pull is to come on both standing parts. It makes a good sling or boatswain's chair, because a double loop is more comfortable to sit in than a single loop. To tie it, pass the bight B up through the hitch A (Fig. 19A). Enlarge B and fold it down over A and C. Bring B up behind the knot, and adjust the loop C to the desired size (Fig. 19B). The finished knot is shown in Fig. 19C.

FIG. 17A

FIG. 17B

FIG. 18A

FIG. 18B

FIG. 18C

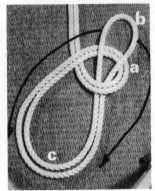

FIG. 19A

FIG. 19B

FIG. 19C

20. The **PORTUGUESE BOWLINE** also has a double loop (see No. 19), but it is tied in the end of a line rather than in the bight. Riesenberg calls it the French bowline, and describes in his book *Under Sail* how a French sailor taught it to him. To tie it by Riesenberg's method, start as if tying an ordinary bowline. Then, before passing the end round behind the standing part, make another loop *B*, and bring the end up through the cuckold's neck. To complete the knot, pass the end round behind the standing part, and down through the cuckold's neck, as shown by the arrow (Fig. 20A).

When the knot is used as a sling, a man can either sit in both loops (Fig. 20B), or he can sit in *A* and bring *B* (Fig. 20C) round his back and under his armpits, with the knot pressed against his chest.

21. The **SPANISH BOWLINE** has two adjustable loops which can be fitted over two objects, such as the two legs of a ladder, when a ladder is slung horizontally as a scaffold. Since the loops are adjustable, they can also slip. Therefore a scaffold supported by a Spanish bowline must be used with caution. The Spanish bowline can also be used as a boatswain's chair, with the loops fitted over a man's legs.

To tie it, form three loops, as shown in Fig. 21A. Turn the large centre loop *AB* down, as shown by the arrow. Enlarge *AB* until it covers loops *C* and *D* (Fig. 21C). Finally push bights *A* and *B* up through loops *C* and *D*. The finished knot is shown in Fig. 21D. There are several other ways to tie the Spanish bowline.

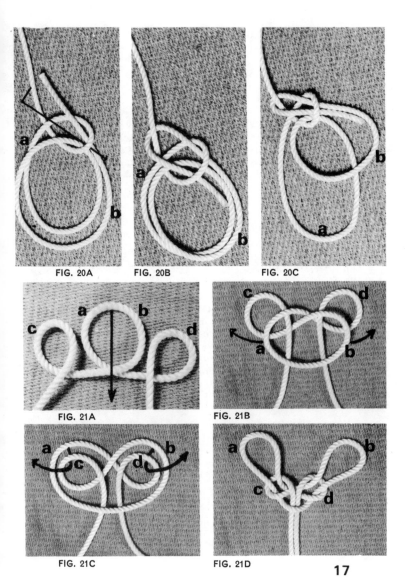

FIG. 20A   FIG. 20B   FIG. 20C

FIG. 21A

FIG. 21B

FIG. 21C

FIG. 21D

17

22. The **RUNNING BOWLINE** consists of a bowline tied round the standing part. It is the sailor's most useful temporary noose or running knot.

23. The **OVERHAND RUNNING KNOT** or **NOOSE** is the simplest of several temporary running knots or slip knots. To tie it, form a loop *A*, thrust the hand through *A*, grasp the standing part at *B*, and bring *B* back through *A* (Fig. 23A). This noose is rather insecure. To make it more secure, tie an overhand knot in the end.

24. The **OVERHAND LOOP** or **LOOP KNOT** is the most convenient way to tie a fixed loop in the end of a piece of thread, twine or marline. It should not be used in rope, however, because it jams and cannot be readily untied. Knots tied in rope, which is expensive, generally have to be untied when they have served their purpose, so that the rope can be used again. Knots tied in thread, twine or marline, which is comparatively cheap, can usually be cut off and discarded when they are no longer needed. Hence a knot that is appropriate in one material is sometimes quite inappropriate in another material.

The overhand loop cannot shake loose and become untied. The bowline, structurally a better knot, can. When there is danger of its doing so, the end of a bowline should always be stopped (see Glossary) to the standing part.

25. The **FISHERMAN'S LOOP, ENGLISHMAN'S LOOP** or **TRUE-LOVER'S KNOT** is hardly a sailor's knot, though all sailors are familiar with it. It looks strong, but actually has a low breaking strength. It is often recommended in mountaineering books, probably unwisely, as an end loop for the climbing rope. To tie it, form two loops (Fig. 25A), and bring a bight *A* down through *B*. The finished knot, when pulled taut, has two overhand knots which fit snugly together and cannot slip (hence, perhaps, the name true-lover's knot).

FIG. 22   FIG. 23A   FIG. 23B

FIG. 24   FIG. 25A   FIG. 25B

5 Hitches and similar knots

26. The **MIDSHIPMAN'S HITCH** is a strong, semi-permanent loop which cannot jam. It is based on the rolling hitch (No. 40). It holds well as long as the end is kept in contact with the standing part. This can be achieved by means of a light seizing (see Nos. 48 and 49) as illustrated, or (for very temporary purposes) by means of the hand alone. This is perhaps the only practicable knot to tie if you are overboard, and have hold of the end of a line that has been thrown to you, particularly if you are being pulled through the water at a rapid speed.

27. The **HALF HITCH AND SEIZING** is similar to No. 26, but it is not quite so secure.

28. The **BUNTLINE HITCH** was formerly used to secure the buntlines to the foot of the sail on square riggers. Since the second half hitch is nipped or jammed inside the first when the knot is drawn taut, it is a very safe knot. Four-in-hand neckties are usually tied with a buntline hitch.

29. The **CATSPAW** is used to hitch a sling to a hook. To tie it, twist the two loops *A* and *B* (Fig. 29A) in opposite directions, and place them on the hook (Fig. 29B). The catspaw cannot possibly jam. It functions best when the pull comes on both standing parts.

30. The **BLACKWALL HITCH** is a quick but insecure way to hitch a line to a hook. It holds only as long as the tension is maintained; therefore it should be used only for temporary purposes, as when securing a tackle to a line that is to be hauled on. It should never be used for lifting heavy loads, or when damage would result if it slipped. To tie it, bring a hitch up over the hook from beneath (Fig. 30A), and drop the end in place first, and then the standing part (Fig. 30B).

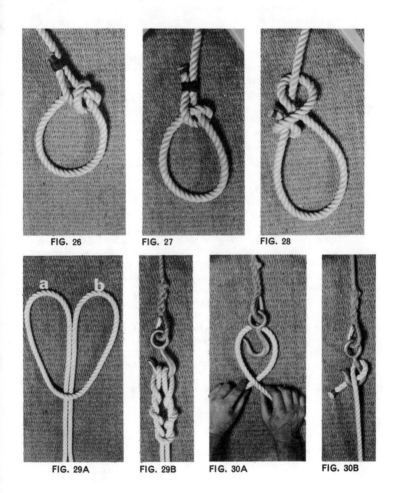

FIG. 26   FIG. 27   FIG. 28

FIG. 29A   FIG. 29B   FIG. 30A   FIG. 30B

31. The **SHEEPSHANK** is used about as often as the crossbow, according to Captain Riesenberg. Formerly, however, it was a very important knot, and Captain John Smith, of Virginia, mentioned it in 1627 (along with the wall knot and the bowline) as one of the three knots then used by seamen. Its function is to shorten a line temporarily, and it holds only as long as a steady pull is maintained. For more permanent purposes, the bights *A* and *B* can be seized or stopped (see Glossary) to the standing parts.

32. The **LARK'S HEAD** or **COW HITCH** is a good knot to use when the pull comes on both parts. It is familiar on keys, baggage tags, and the like. In structure it is identical with No. 84.

33. The **LARK'S HEAD WITH TOGGLE** is released instantly upon the withdrawal of the toggle.

34. TWO HALF HITCHES are often used to hitch a line temporarily to a ring, post or other object. The two hitches should be tied in the same way (Fig. 34A) and not in opposite ways (Fig. 34B).

35. The **ROUND TURN AND HALF HITCH** is similar to No. 34. The end may be secured with a seizing (Fig. 35), or with an additional half hitch, or with both. "There's a lot of virtue in a round turn," according to an old saying. And indeed a surprising amount of additional security is provided by the extra turn round the ring or post. A round turn and two half hitches are also an effective combination.

36. The **FISHERMAN'S BEND** or **ANCHOR BEND** holds well on either ring or spar, has a high breaking strength, and cannot slip or jam. The end may be seized or stopped to the standing part, as in Fig. 36A, or secured to the standing part with a half hitch, as in Fig. 36B.

The fisherman's bend is shown in Fig. 36B secured to a spar instead of to a ring. The end is hitched to the standing part. Another way to secure the end is to tie it to the standing part with a bowline.

FIG. 31

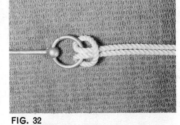

FIG. 32

FIG. 33

FIG. 34A

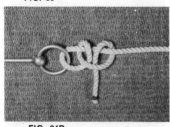

FIG. 34B

FIG. 35

FIG. 36A

FIG. 36B

37. The **STUDDINGSAIL HALYARD BEND** is exactly like the fisherman's bend except that the end is tucked back under the first turn (Fig. 37A). It is an excellent hitch, with a high breaking strength, and little tendency to slip. A form with an additional turn round the spar (Fig. 37B) is pictured in a number of books under the name "topsail halyard bend."

38. The **CLOVE HITCH** or **RATLINE HITCH** is used in making a painter fast to a post or piling, in securing the ratlines to the shrouds, and for many other purposes. To tie it in a quick way, throw a single hitch (see Glossary) over the post (Fig. 38A), holding the standing part in one hand, and the end in the other. Let go the standing part, and with the end of the line (which should be left long enough for the purpose) throw a second hitch over the post (Fig. 38B). The finished knot is shown in Fig. 38C. When you cannot reach the top of the post, pass the end twice round in such a way as to form the hitch. For permanent security, stop the end to the standing part, or hitch it to the standing part with two half hitches.

39. The **TIMBER HITCH** or **LOG HITCH** is useful when towing or lifting a log or spar. It has a very high breaking strength, and cannot possibly jam. In tying the timber hitch, be sure to "dog" the end "with the lay," or in other words, twist the end round the other part in the same direction as the twist of the spiral strands (Fig. 39A). A half hitch some distance away from the knot will help to keep the spar or log in line (Fig. 39B).

FIG. 37A   FIG. 37B

FIG. 38A

FIG. 38B

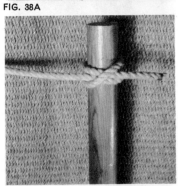

FIG. 38C

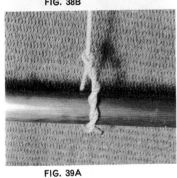

FIG. 39A

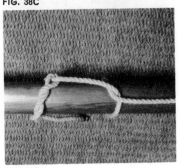

FIG. 39B

FIG. 40A   FIG. 40B   FIG. 40C

40. The **ROLLING HITCH** or **STOPPER HITCH** is used to secure a small line to a larger line when the strain is expected to be parallel or nearly parallel to the axis of the larger line. To tie it, pass the end round the larger line (Fig. 40A), and then pass it round again, making sure that the second turn is jammed inside the first (Fig. 40B). It is now necessary to dispose of the end, and there are several ways to do so. One way is to stop it to the larger line (Fig. 40C), or (for very temporary purposes) to hold it against the larger line while the hitch is in use. Another way is to take a hitch round the larger line, and then to back the end round against the lay several times before stopping it (Fig. 40D). This method is recommended in the British Admiralty *Manual of Seamanship*. However, if the hitch marked by the arrow in Fig. 40D is omitted, as it usually is, the end should be "dogged" with the lay and not against it. A third and very common method is to continue the end round and finish it off with a half hitch and nothing more (Fig. 40E).

When the rolling hitch is used to secure a line to a spar or post, the second turn is not usually jammed inside the first turn, as described above, and the end is usually either seized to the standing part, or secured with two half hitches. This form of the knot resembles the clove hitch (No. 38), and is sometimes called the magnus hitch or the mooring knot. It will bear a strain either parallel or perpendicular to the spar (Fig. 40F).

41. The **TOM FOOL KNOT** is a trick knot without any practical applications. One way to tie it is grasp *AB* in one hand, and *CD* in the other (Fig. 41A), and join them with an overhand knot (Fig. 41B).

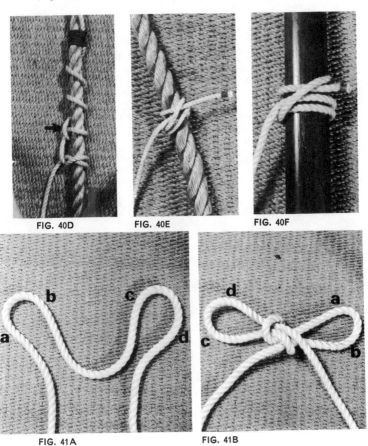

FIG. 40D   FIG. 40E   FIG. 40F

FIG. 41A   FIG. 41B

42. SINGLE JUG SLING or **ROPE HANDCUFFS.** Lay down two loops, as shown in Fig. 42A, and pull *B* and *C* apart. (If the second loop is laid down under the first loop, instead of on top of it, the result will be a Tom Fool knot.) To use the jug sling for handcuffs, place the prisoner's hands in the two loops (Fig. 42B), draw the knot taut round the wrists, and tie the ends together with a square knot. To use it as a jug or bottle sling, place the neck of the bottle in the centre of the knot, tie the ends together with a square knot, and lift the bottle with the two loops.

43. JUG SLING or **HACKAMORE.** Lay down two loops as in Fig. 43A. Form a bight at *A*, and pass it under *B*, over *C*, under *D* and over *E*. Fold loop *EE* back and down as shown by the arrow in Fig. 43B. Fold loop *F* forward and down, as shown by the arrow in Fig. 43C. Fit the neck of the jar or bottle into the centre of the knot, adjust the parts snugly, tie the two ends together with a square knot, and carry the bottle by means of the loop *A* and the loop formed by the two knotted ends.

This is an astonishingly secure and ingenious knot. It will lift the heaviest and most slippery bottle, even if the rim or flange is almost imperceptible. In America in the west it goes under the name hackamore, and is said to be used as a temporary rope bridle. There are several different methods of trying it. It was known to the ancient Greeks and Romans.

FIG. 42A

FIG. 42B

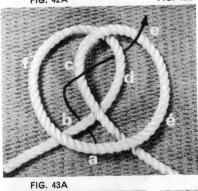

FIG. 43A

FIG. 43B

FIG. 43C

FIG. 43D

44. The **JURY KNOT** or **MASTHEAD KNOT.** Lay down three loops, as shown in Fig. 44A. Pull *C* to the left under *B* and over *A*. Pull *D* to the right, over *E* and under *F*. Tie *H* and *J* together with a bowline knot. Place the centre of the knot over the masthead, and bend stays to the three bights *C*, *D* and *G* (Fig. 44B). The standing part (either *H* or *J*) will presumably be long enough to serve as a fourth stay. The jury mast can now be stayed by means of four stays (Fig. 44C).

A jury mast is a makeshift mast rigged at sea to replace a mast that has been carried away in a storm. Whether the masthead knot has ever actually been used to stay a jury mast I cannot say. It is, however, an ingenious knot, and well worth knowing. There are three varieties of the knot, which differ slightly as a result of different ways in which the three loops (Fig. 44A) can be laid down.

The knot can also be used as a bottle sling, with the four bights as handles. It is probably as good as No. 43 for this purpose, but more troublesome to adjust.

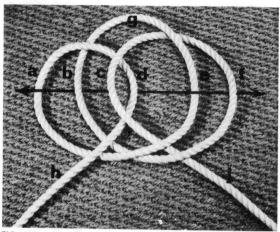

FIG. 44A

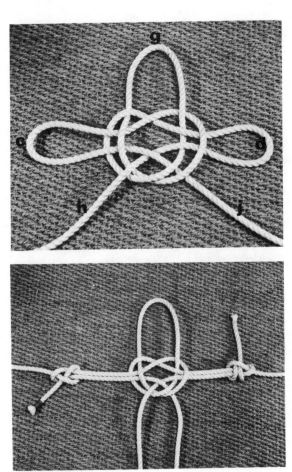

FIGS. 44B and 44C

6 Belaying

45. BELAYING means making a line fast by winding it figure-eight fashion round a cleat, belaying pin or pair of bitts.

Begin by taking a turn round the pin (Fig. 45A) or cleat (Fig. 45D) before the figure-eight turns are laid on (Fig. 45B). In belaying on a cleat, be sure to lead the standing part *S* to the far end of the cleat, as in Fig. 45D, and *not* to the near end, as in Fig. 45E.

As for the way to conclude the operation, much has been written about the dangers of a final hitch, as in Fig. 45F. And on very small sailboats it is usually unwise to clinch the sheets, and possibly also the halyards, in this manner. On the other hand, a final hitch is sometimes perfectly safe, and even necessary.

As a matter of fact no general rule can be laid down, since each situation has to be judged on its own merits. A slipped hitch (Fig. 45C) has been suggested as a solution to the problem, but is not wholly satisfactory. When a final hitch is permitted, it should follow the lay, as in Fig. 45F, and not be laid on in the lopsided fashion shown in Fig. 45G.

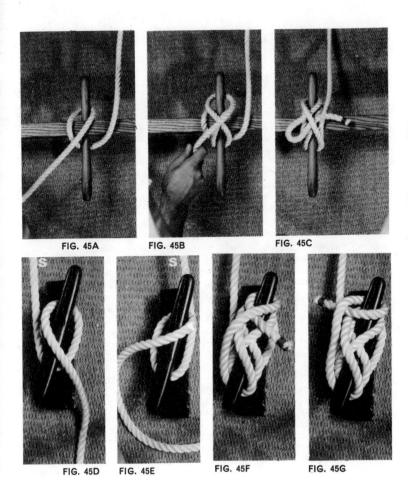

FIG. 45A   FIG. 45B   FIG. 45C

FIG. 45D   FIG. 45E   FIG. 45F   FIG. 45G

33

7 Whipping

46. PLAIN WHIPPING. A whipping is a small lashing put on the end of a rope to prevent it from unravelling and becoming unlaid. The material most commonly used is sail twine, but for the sake of photographic clarity a heavier stuff is used in the illustrations on the opposite page. To put on a plain whipping, wind or wrap the twine against the lay of the rope, and work towards the end of the rope. Draw each turn taut as it is put on. Take the last few turns over the free end of the twine (Figs. 46B and 46C). Then pull the end through to the left and cut it off close (Fig. 46D). Finally cut or seal the end of the rope near the whipping, but not too near. The whipping in the illustration (Fig. 46D) is too long in proportion to the diameter of the rope, owing to the thickness of the twine that is used. The length of a whipping should be about equal to the diameter of the rope.

47. PALM-AND-NEEDLE WHIPPING is the neatest and most permanent method. It is made with the help of a sailor's palm and a sail needle. Wax the twine with beeswax, stitch it through the rope (Fig. 47A), and take several turns round both the rope and the end of the twine (Fig. 47A, lower picture), just as in plain whipping. Stitch the twine through again, and carry it back to the left, over the whipping, and along the spiral groove between the strands (Fig. 47B, upper picture). Stitch the twine through a third time, carry it to the right along a second spiral groove, and stitch it through once more (Fig. 47B, lower picture). Repeat this process, working back and forth from left to right and from right to left, until all the spiral cross turns (see Glossary) are *doubled*. Finally stitch the twine through once or twice more, and cut it off. (The doubling of the cross turns could not be pictured in Fig. 47B owing to the heavy stuff that was used in place of twine in the specimen.)

Synthetic ropes and lines can be sealed either by burning the ends with a match or red-hot knife, or else by heat shrinking proprietary sleeves over the end.

FIG. 46A

FIG. 46B

FIG. 46C

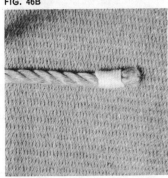

FIG. 46D

FIG. 47A

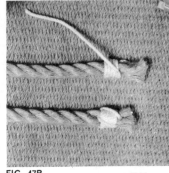

FIG. 47B

8 Seizings

48. The **ROUND SEIZING** is a lashing used to hold two ropes, or two parts of the same rope, together.

To "clap on" a round seizing, heave the two parts together, by means of a Spanish windlass (No. 50) if necessary. Splice a small eye in the seizing stuff, which should be well stretched in advance, and then pass the end round both ropes and up through the eye (Fig. 48A). Take six to ten turns round both ropes, and bring the end back through the eye again (Fig. 48B). Heave each turn taut. Lay on a second series of turns, called riders or riding turns, but not so taut as to separate the turns of the first layer. Push the end of the seizing stuff down between the last two turns of the first layer (Fig. 48C).

Take two cross turns, or frapping turns, to hold the turns of the seizing in place, and to tighten them; and secure the cross turns with a clove hitch (Figs. 48D and 48E). Dispose of the end by taking three or four turns round one of the ropes, and seizing it with a very small seizing (Fig. 48F), or by securing it with two half-hitches (not illustrated).

A seizing with cross turns but without riders or riding turns is called a flat seizing (not illustrated).

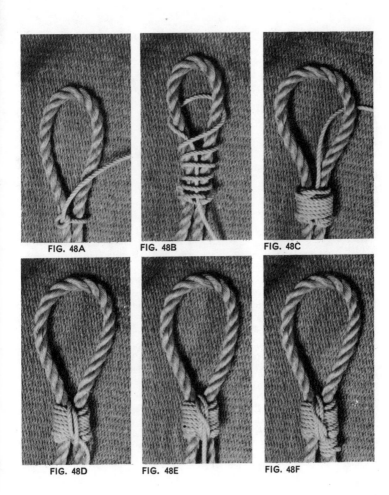

FIG. 48A   FIG. 48B   FIG. 48C

FIG. 48D   FIG. 48E   FIG. 48F

FIG. 48G   FIG. 48H   FIG. 49

48 (*continued*). The **ROUND SEIZING.** Fig. 48G shows another way to begin a round seizing. After the first layer of turns has been put on, pass the end of the seizing stuff up under one turn only, instead of under all the turns as in Fig. 48B. Then lay the riding turns on as before, and secure them with cross turns.

Fig. 48H shows another way to secure the cross turns. Here the end of the seizing stuff is brought up between the two cross turns, which are then hove taut, and a wall knot (No. 54) is worked in the end.

49. The **RACKING SEIZING** is used when excessive tension is expected on one of the parts. The turns are passed figure-eight fashion, and then each turn is hove taut with a marline spike (see No. 51). Ten or fifteen turns are customary. The turns of the second layer fit between the turns of the first layer (not illustrated). Cross turns are put on, just as in a round seizing.

FIG. 50

FIG. 51A

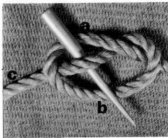

FIG. 51B

50. The **SPANISH WINDLASS** is an old device for exerting power when heaving the two parts of a rope together for any purpose. It is made as illustrated in Fig. 50, with a well-greased line, a steel bar, and two marline spikes. It was used in the days of the sailing ship when putting on a "throat" seizing.

51. The **MARLINE-SPIKE HITCH** can be instantly tied and instantly released. It is useful when increased power or leverage is needed to heave a line taut, as in "clapping on" a seizing. Fold *AB* down over *C*, and slip the marline spike under *C*. Grasp the marline spike in the hand and pull on the line directly; or rest the spike on a fixed point as a fulcrum, and use it as a lever.

9 End or stopper knots

52. The **CROWN KNOT** is never used alone, but always as part of other knots. Unlay the rope a short distance, form a bight in one of the strands (Fig. 52A), and stick the end of the next strand down through this bight (Fig. 52B). Stick the end of the third strand down through the bight of the second strand, and the end of the first strand down through the bight of the third strand. Work the strands taut (Fig. 52C). It is perhaps simpler to describe the process thus: the end of each strand goes down through the bight of the next strand.

53. The **BACK SPLICE** is a way—a rather clumsy and unattractive way—of finishing off the end of a rope. First crown the rope (No. 52) as described above. Then tuck each strand over and under against the lay, as in making a short splice or an eye splice (Nos. 72 and 73). Tuck each strand again, and cut off the ends. Fig. 53 shows a back splice after each strand has been tucked twice, but before the ends have been trimmed.

54. The **WALL KNOT** is the converse of the crown knot. Each strand comes up through the bight of the next strand (Fig. 54A). Work the strands taut (Fig. 54B), lay the strands up again above the knot, whip them'(No. 46), and cut off the ends (Fig. 54C). The wall knot is used as a stopper knot (see Glossary), to finish off seizings (see No. 48, Fig. 48H) and in tying other knots (see No. 78).

FIG. 52A   **FIG. 52B**   **FIG. 52C**   **FIG. 53**

FIG. 54A   FIG. 54B   FIG. 54C

55. The **DOUBLE WALL KNOT.** Tie a wall knot, but before working the strands taut follow the lead with each strand until it comes out on top of the knot. Lay the strands up again above the knot, whip them and cut off the ends (Fig. 55).

56. The **WALL-AND-CROWN KNOT** is used chiefly as the basis of the double-wall-and-crown. To tie it, first tie a wall knot, and then tie a crown knot (Nos. 54 and 52).

FIG. 55   FIG. 56

57. The **DOUBLE-WALL-AND-CROWN KNOT** or **MAN-ROPE KNOT** is made from a wall-and-crown (No. 56). Before working the strands taut, follow round the wall with each strand, and then follow round the crown with each strand. Work the knot taut and cut off the ends of the strands (Fig. 57).

58. The **DIAMOND KNOT** is similar to the wall knot, except that each strand comes up, not through the bight of the next strand, but through the bight of the next strand but one (Fig. 58A). Work the knot taut, lay up the strands above the knot and whip the end (Fig. 58B).

FIG. 57   FIG. 58A   FIG. 58B

59. The **DOUBLE DIAMOND KNOT.** Tie a single diamond knot (No. 58) and with each strand follow the lead of the adjacent strand until all the strands come out on top of the knot. Work taut, lay up the strands, and whip the end (Fig. 59).

60. The **MATTHEW WALKER KNOT** is similar to the wall knot, except that each strand comes up through the bights of the next two strands (Fig. 60A), instead of through the bight of the next strand. One way to tie it is to begin with a wall knot (No. 54). Then before working the knot taut bring the end of each strand up through the bight of one more strand. To finish the knot, lay up the strands and whip the end (Fig. 60B).

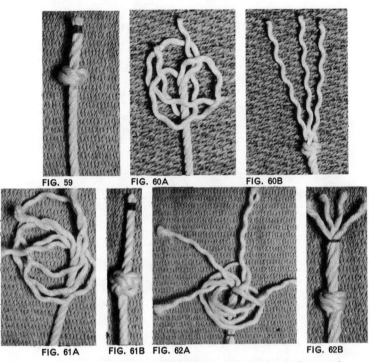

FIG. 59 FIG. 60A FIG. 60B

FIG. 61A FIG. 61B FIG. 62A FIG. 62B

61. The **DOUBLE MATTHEW WALKER** is similar to the Matthew Walker (No. 60), except that each strand comes up through the next three bights (Fig. 61A) instead of through the next two bights. The finished knot (Fig. 61B) is the most attractive of the multi-strand stopper knots.

62. The **LANYARD KNOT** is a Matthew Walker (No. 60) tied in four-strand rope. It was used as a stopper knot in the days of hemp shrouds to prevent the lanyards from unreeving through the deadeyes. The reader should consult a nautical dictionary or a nineteenth century manual of seamanship if he is in doubt about the meaning of any of the terms in the preceding sentence.

10 A knot for the heaving line

63. The **MONKEY'S FIST** or **MONKEY FIST** is a knob used to weight the end of a heaving line. To tie it, form three loops (Fig. 63A). Pass the end *B* three times round these loops (Fig. 63B). Pass the end through the first set of loops in the manner indicated by the arrow (Fig. 63B). Pass the end three times round the second set of loops (Fig. 63C). Work the loops gradually taut (Fig. 63D). Splice the end to the standing part (Fig. 63E). A weight (not so heavy as to be dangerous) can be placed inside the knob before the turns are worked taut. Two turns can be taken instead of three if a smaller knob is desired.

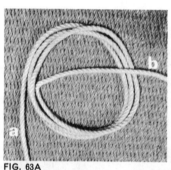

FIG. 63A

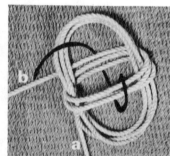

FIG. 63B

FIG. 63C

FIG. 63D

FIG. 63E

11 Turk's head

64. The **RUNNING TURK'S HEAD** is an ornamental lashing used as a grip or handhold on a tiller, stanchion, etc. To tie a knot of three strands and five bights, pass the end around as in Fig. 64A. Rotate the knot until the crossing becomes visible and tuck to the right beyond the crossing as in Fig. 64B. Push a small loop to the right as in Fig. 64C. Tuck to the left as in Fig. 64D and E. The knot is now complete. Fig. 64K shows this knot with the strands doubled (specimen *A*) and tripled (specimen *B*).

A knot of four strands and three bights can be tied as in Figs. 64F–J. Fig. 64K (Specimen *C*) shows this knot with strands tripled.

FIG. 64A   FIG. 64B   FIG. 64C   FIG. 64D

FIG. 64E   FIG. 64F   FIG. 64G   FIG. 64H

FIG. 64J   FIG. 64K

12 Six useful knots

66. The **BUTTERFLY KNOT** or **LINEMAN'S RIDER** is the best middleman's knot for mountain climbers. Unlike the artillery or man-harness knot, it cannot be unintentionally pulled out of shape and transformed into a slip noose, and unlike the true-lover's knot (No. 25), it cannot jam. Like the bowline, it can be readily untied after a strain. It fits round the climber's chest and can be hauled on from either direction.

67. The **CONSTRICTOR KNOT** is indispensable as a temporary whipping, as a clamp when two pieces of wood are being glued together, and for all sorts of odd jobs and household repairs. It grips cylindrical objects like a boa constrictor, but (important warning) it does not hold on corners or flat surfaces. It makes a good miller's knot to tie up the mouth of a sack.

68. The **STANLEY BARNES KNOT,** an angler's knot, is preferable to the more familiar "perfection knot" when a loop is needed in the end of a nylon cast, leader or spinning line. It is strong, safe, easy to remember, and well streamlined. Note that it is tied with half a turn more than a figure-eight loop knot.

69. The **TURTLE KNOT** is an old and reliable way to tie a cast or leader to a hook or fly. It is safe in either gut or nylon monofil.

70. The **BLOOD KNOT** (English nomenclature) or **BARREL KNOT** (American nomenclature) is the best way to tie the ends of two nylon casts or leaders together. There are several variations in the technique of tying it.

71. The **PERFECT KNOT** (so named because it is nearly perfect) is recommended by Dr. Barnes in his authoritative *Anglers' Knots in Gut and Nylon* (Birmingham, 1951) as the best way to tie a nylon cast to a swivel. Pass the turns successively over the eye, beginning with the outside turn (Fig. 71A). Pull taut and cut the end off short (Fig. 71B).

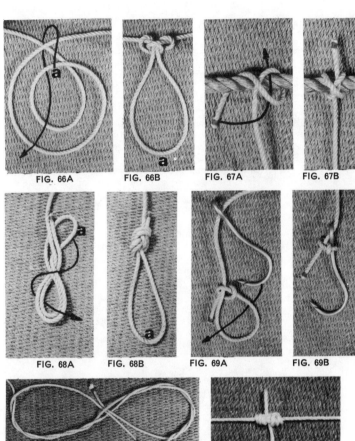

FIG. 66A FIG. 66B FIG. 67A FIG. 67B

FIG. 68A FIG. 68B FIG. 69A FIG. 69B

FIG. 70A FIG. 70B

FIG. 71A FIG. 71B

13 Splicing

72. The **SHORT SPLICE** is stronger than the long splice (No. 74), but it increases the diameter of the rope, so that it cannot be run over a sheave or through a block.

Unlay the strands of the two ropes a short distance, and crotch them (Fig. 72A). Stop down one set of strands temporarily. Beginning with any strand of the other set, tuck it against the lay, over one strand and under one strand of the opposite rope (Figs. 72B and 72C). Tuck the two remaining strands in the same manner (Fig. 72D). Remove the stop and tuck the second set of strands into the first rope, in each case over and under one as before (Fig. 72E). Use a marline spike or fid, if necessary, to force an opening between the strands. Then tuck each strand once or twice more, over one and under one, against the lay.

Roll the splice under foot, and pound it with a marline spike, to ensure an even adjustment of the strands. Do not cut the ends off too close or they will be apt to work out. The finished splice should look like the lower specimen in Fig. 72F.

A tapered effect, as in the upper specimen in Fig. 72F, can be secured by halving the strands before the final tuck, and by trimming the ends close. This, however, is a practice of doubtful value.

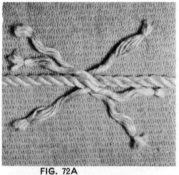

FIG. 72A

FIG. 72B

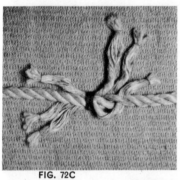

FIG. 72C

FIG. 72D

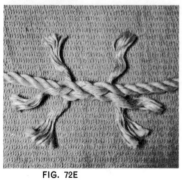

FIG. 72E

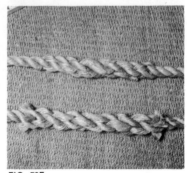

FIG. 72F

73. The **EYE SPLICE** is more frequently used than any other splice. Unlay the strands a sufficient distance. Tuck the middle strand *A* under one strand, against the lay, at the desired point (Fig. 73A). Tuck *B* under the next strand (Fig. 73B). Turn the work over, and tuck *C* under the remaining strand (Fig. 73C). It is important to tuck all three strands at the same point longitudinally along the rope.

Tuck each strand a second time (Fig. 73D). Tuck each strand a third time (Fig. 73E, the first specimen). Do not cut the strands off too close or they may work out when the rope is stretched. When a splice is to be served with twine (No. 77), the strands may be halved before the last tuck in order to give the splice a tapered appearance, as shown in Fig. 73E, the second specimen. The service will prevent the strands from working out.

An eye splice in four-strand rope can be made exactly as described above, except that after the work has been turned over for the first time the last *two* strands are tucked (under one strand each). An alternative method is to tuck strand *B* under two strands the first time it is tucked, as illustrated in Fig. 73F. Then turn the work over, and tuck the two remaining strands under one strand each. Proceed as with three-strand rope.

The strands of synthetic ropes and lines may be sealed with a match or red-hot knife. Take care not to burn through the rope where the loose strands emerge between the lay or the splice will be seriously weakened. It is best to leave a small stub with a sealed end exposed for about one eighth or one quarter of an inch.

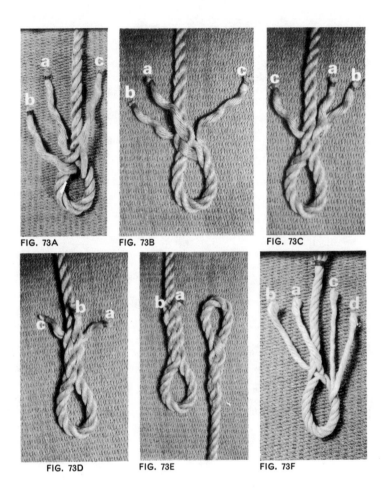

FIG. 73A   FIG. 73B   FIG. 73C

FIG. 73D   FIG. 73E   FIG. 73F

74. The **LONG SPLICE** is weaker than the short splice and requires more rope, but it does not increase the diameter appreciably. Unlay the strands several times farther than the photographs indicate, and crotch them (Fig. 74A). Unlay *A* still farther, and lay up *D* in the groove vacated by *A*. Do the same thing in the opposite direction with *B* and *E*. The result will be three pairs of strands meeting at three different points (Fig. 74B).

The problem now is to dispose of the strands. If the diameter of the splice must be as small as possible, halve each strand (for example *A* and *D*), and join half of *A* with half of *D* by means of a half-knot (Fig. 74C). The unknotted halves of *A* and *D* can be cut off later.

If a slight increase in diameter is permissible, knot the pairs of strands without halving them (for example *B* and *E* in Fig. 74C). After being knotted, the strands are then tucked into the rope. One way to do this is to tuck them against the lay, over one and under one, several times. Another method is to tuck the strands with the lay. By this method each strand is, in effect, wrapped spirally round and round a strand in the other rope. In Fig. 74C strands *F* and *C* have been halved and knotted, and the unknotted halves have been cut off. In Fig. 74D, strands *F* and *C* have been tucked and cut off; strands *A* and *D* have been halved and knotted, and tucked once each. The ends of the strands should not be cut off too close, or they may work out.

75. The **CHAIN SPLICE.** Reeve two strands, *A* and *B*, through the end link (Fig. 75A), and tuck *B* under *A*, against the lay (Fig. 75A). Unlay *C* a considerable distance, and lay up *A* in the groove vacated by *C*. Knot *A* and *C* together with a half-knot (Fig. 75B), and dispose of them by tucking them either with or against the lay, as in making a *long* splice. Tuck *B* over and under against the lay, as in making a *short* splice.

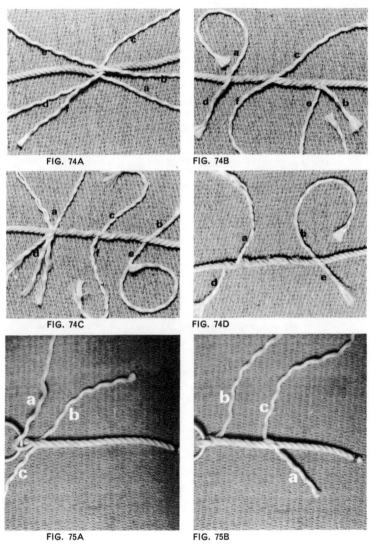

FIG. 74A

FIG. 74B

FIG. 74C

FIG. 74D

FIG. 75A

FIG. 75B

53

14 Miscellaneous operations

76. The **MARLING HITCH** consists of a series of hitches round an object, such as parcelling (No. 77), to hold it in place. The verb "to marl" means to secure with marling hitches.

77. WORMING, PARCELLING and **SERVING** are three operations intended to protect a rope from chafe or dampness. The rope to be treated should be stretched taut about waist high. To worm, fill the spiral grooves with marline, spun yarn or other stuff of suitable diameter, working with the lay.

This is to make the rope smooth and cylindrical before parcelling.

Parcelling consists of strips of canvas, often waterproofed with tar or by some other means, laid on over the worming, and marled (No. 76) in place. Over this is put the service.

Serving is done with a serving mallet and marline or other twine. The service is always put on against the lay of the rope, the worming and parcelling with the lay. An old mnemonic couplet, handed down from the days when every sailor had to know how to worm, parcel and serve, runs as follows:

> Worm and parcel with the lay;
> Turn and serve the other way

78. The **SHROUD KNOT** is part knot and part splice. Unlay the strands a short distance, and crotch them. With each set of strands, make a wall knot (No. 54) round the opposite rope, preferably against the lay (Fig. 78A). To dispose of the ends, separate them into yarns. Scrape them down with a knife. Then marl (see No. 76), parcel and serve (see No. 77). The finished knot (Fig. 78C) presents a neat appearance. The shroud knot was formerly used to repair hemp shrouds which had been shot or carried away.

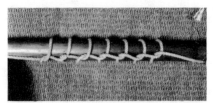
FIG. 76

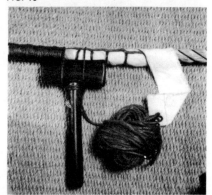
FIG. 77

FIG. 78A

FIG. 78B

FIG. 78C

79. The **SPINDLE EYE SPLICE.** Whip the rope, unlay the strands, and separate the strands into yarns. Divide the yarns into two equal groups, and half-knot them together, one pair at a time, round a spindle of the required diameter (Fig. 79A). In knotting the yarns be sure to scatter the knots round the spindle. With several lengths of marline, bind the yarns tightly in place (Fig. 79B). This can be done most easily if several lengths of marline are laid out on the spindle before the yarns are knotted. Scrape down and taper the ends of the yarns, and serve (see No. 77) with marline (Fig. 79C).

80. The **CRINGLE** is made round a thimble in the bolt-rope of a sail. Reeve the ends of the strand through the eyelet-holes in the sail (Fig. 80A). Lay the strand up on itself, and reeve the ends through the eyelet-holes once more (Fig. 80B). Lay the strands up a second time, until they meet at the top of the cringle (Fig. 80C). The cringle will then have the thickness of four strands. Work the strands taut, until the hole is somewhat smaller than the thimble. Stretch the cringle by hammering a fid into the hole. Insert the thimble quickly upon withdrawing the fid, allow the cringle to shrink down on the thimble, and cut off the ends of the strands (Fig. 80D).

81. The **GROMMET** is made with a strand which should be more than three times as long as the circumference of the grommet. Lay this strand up on itself in the form of a circle, and when the ends come together, halve them, join them with a half-knot, and tuck them as in making a long splice (see No. 74). Sometimes with very small grommets the strands are knotted without being halved and tucked, and are then cut off close and varnished to make the grommet hard and secure. Grommets are used for the handles of chests, for quoits, and for strops (see No. 83).

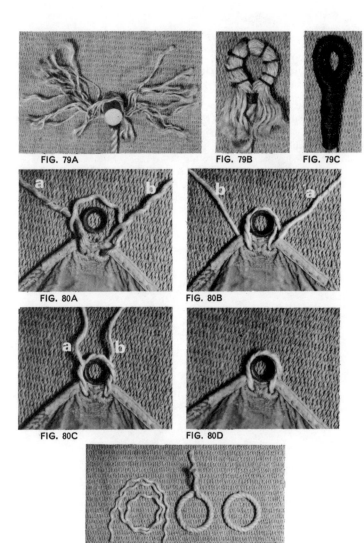

FIG. 79A

FIG. 79B

FIG. 79C

FIG. 80A

FIG. 80B

FIG. 80C

FIG. 80D

FIG. 81

57

82. The **SELVAGEE STRAP** is made by passing several turns of small stuff round two pegs or spikes set the desired distance apart. When enough turns have been taken, the ends are spliced or knotted together, and temporary stops are put on to hold the strands in place. The strap is then firmly marled (see No. 76), and the spikes are removed. Figs. 82A and 82B show two ways in which a strap can be used to hook a tackle to a spar (Fig. 82A) or rope (Fig. 82B).

83. The **GROMMET STRAP** is an endless piece of rope, made either with a single strand (see No. 81), or with a length of rope the ends of which are spliced together. It is used in the same ways as a selvagee strap (No. 82), but is less supple, pliable and strong.

84. The **BALE SLING** is the same knot as the lark's head (No. 32). It can be used to sling bales, sacks, barrels, *etc*. It can be made either with a strap (Nos. 82 and 83), or with a bowline (No. 18).

85. The **BARREL SLING.** Stand the barrel on the rope some distance from the end, and join the end and the standing part with an overhand knot over the top of the barrel. Spread out and separate the overhand knot, and bring the two halves of the knot a short distance down the sides of the barrel. Join the end and the standing part with a bowline knot.

FIG. 82A

FIG. 82B

FIG. 83

FIG. 84

FIG. 85

15 Splicing wire rope

86. The **EYE SPLICE IN WIRE ROPE.** Bend the rope round a pear-shaped thimble two feet or more from the end. For this purpose, a vice, preferably a rigger's vice, is essential. Whip the strands, if the wire is not pre-formed, and unlay them as far as the thimble. Tuck *A* under three strands. Tuck *B* under two strands, entering between the same two strands as *A*. Tuck *C* under one strand, entering between the same two strands as *A* and *B* (Fig. 86A). Turn the work over, replace it in the vice, and tuck *D*, *E* and *F* under one strand each (Fig. 86B). Tuck each strand twice more; then taper and tuck twice again. Each strand in Fig. 86c has been tucked twice. The strands in Fig. 86D have been tucked three times whole, then tapered and tucked, and tapered and tucked again. The strands in Fig. 86E have been tucked twice whole, then tapered and tucked and tapered and tucked again. In tapering, remove about a third of the wires before each tuck.

Tucking with the lay differs from tucking against the lay, for each strand seems to be wrapped spirally round a corresponding strand in the standing part. Except when *A*, *B* and *C* are tucked for the first time, the strands should be untwisted once or twice at each tuck, in order that they may lie flat and become one with the strands about which they are wrapped. When an opening is forced between the strands, the steel spike or pricker should not be inserted at the point where the tuck is desired, but some distance along the rope, away from the thimble. In this way, the strand can be pulled through easily, and at once falls into place when a rotating pressure is exerted on the handle of the spike. The finished splice should be hammered into symmetry, beginning at the thimble, and working towards the standing part.

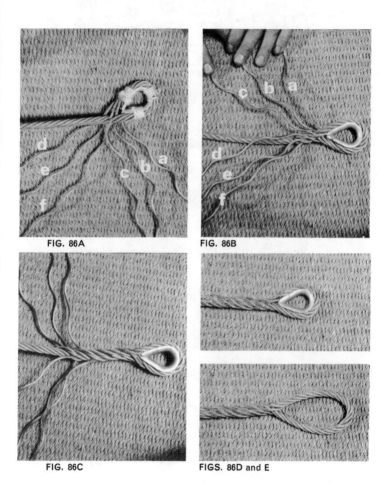

FIG. 86A

FIG. 86B

FIG. 86C

FIGS. 86D and E

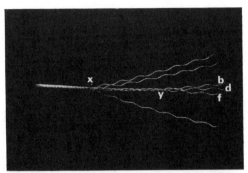

FIG. 87A

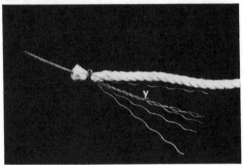

FIG. 87B

87. The **TAIL SPLICE,** for joining fibre rope to wire halyards, *etc.*, is said to have been originated by Nat Herreshoff.

The ends of the wire strands are whipped if necessary. The wire rope is unlaid and the core removed, to point *X*, where it is whipped or secured with a constrictor knot (67B). Alternate strands *B, D* and *F* are then laid together as far as *Y*, and again whipped (Fig. 87A).

The wire is then laid in the groove between any two strands in the fibre rope, and fixed there (Fig. 87B). The long free strands *A, C* and *E* are brought out from the centre of the fibre rope, between the strands at *X*, and the three-strand wire is worked along in the same groove to *Y* (Fig. 87c). Strands *B, D* and *F* are brought out

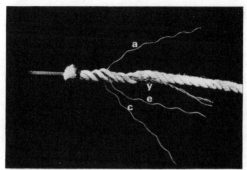

FIG. 87C

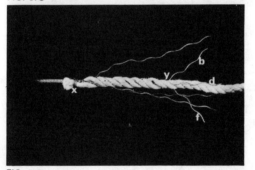

FIG. 87D

between the strands of the rope tail at Y (Fig. 87D).

To dispose of these six wire strands, a grooved or hollow spike is required. With the aid of the spike they are stitched right through the opposing strands of the fibre rope. They may be stitched with or against the lay, but in either case they disappear completely. After each wire strand has been stitched from four to eight times, the ends are cut off close. Where these ends have been cut the splice is parcelled and served. The ends of the fibre strands are combed out, tapered, marled and served, or else heat sealed.

There is a variation of this splice in which the wire strands are tucked over and under the fibre strands.

Index